What This Book Will Do for You

By the end of this book, you'll be able to work through any complex problem—from those that concern only you to those affecting the organization—using generic problem-solving methods that encourage creativity and creative thinking.

Other Titles in the Successful Office Skills Series

Creative
PROBLEM
SOLVING

Donald H. Weiss

amacom
American Management Association

This book is available at a special
discount when ordered in bulk quantities.
For information, contact Special Sales Department,
AMACOM, a division of
American Management Association,
135 West 50th Street, New York, NY 10020.

Library of Congress Cataloging-in-Publication Data

Weiss, Donald H., 1936–
    Creative problem solving.

    (The successful office skills series)
    1. Problem solving. I. Title. II. Series.
HD30.29.W45   1988   658.4   88-47696
ISBN 0-8144-7702-X

Printing number

10 9 8 7 6 5 4 3 2

CONTENTS

Chapter 1

A Case of Broken Eggs: Why You Need to Solve Problems Creatively

The push to include all levels of employees in solving an organization's problems is in full swing. Top management in a growing number of companies wants you and the people reporting to you to participate with them in making operations more productive and to improve the quality of your goods or services.

They want you to solve your own daily problems, such as delegating work to people who'd rather not accept it, handling difficult people, and controlling conflicts. And, they want you to take an active part in solving the kinds of problems they used to reserve to themselves, even though the solutions depended on input from you (which they often didn't seek) and had a direct effect on your work life: planning, quality control, production management.

Now the tide has turned, partly because of Japanese influence, partly because of necessity. You're being asked to cope with tough personal problems, such as overcoming a fear of the automation so many companies are installing, and tough organizational problems, such as increasing production without increasing expenses. Tough problems are being sent back to where they belong: to you and to line employees.

Top management is asking you to grapple with those tough problems, but often it expects you to solve them without showing you how. Maybe that's one of the reasons that "all the king's horses and all the king's men/Couldn't put Humpty Dumpty together again." A lack of leadership and know-how.

Poor Humpty Dumpty. Did you ever wonder why all those horses and men couldn't do the job or do it right?

Sure, he was an egg and yes, there were too many horses and men trying to solve the problem. But in many cases, "horses and men," either singly or in large groups, in many times and in many ways, have been able to put broken eggs back together again.

We repair some so well that if we see the seams at all, we can barely make them out. But other repair jobs resemble the rugged features of lunar craters.

And, we often sit staring helplessly at broken eggs, apparently no more competent to put them back together than were the king's horses and men.

Maybe our impotence comes from trying to arrive at a solution without finding out what broke the egg or how best to put it back together. We look at it, grab the glue pot, slap it together, and put it back on the wall—only to watch it fall off again.

By the time we see that we went about the whole thing all wrong and call in the king's troops, it's too late. They set to work, and by the time they're done, whatever it is, it isn't an egg any more.

Well, by the end of this little book, you'll be in a better position to fix bedevilling eggs (our metaphor for problems), identify the kind of broken eggs they are, understand what makes them break, and learn the proper kinds of tools you need to make them whole again.

You'll be able to work through any complex problem by distinguishing between symptoms and problems, self-centered and organizational-centered problems, analytic and diffuse problems, and vertical and lateral thinking. You'll use generic problem-solving methods that encourage creativity and creative thinking for attacking a real situation of your own.

There are those who may say, "Hey! It's just an egg. Buy another one."

Maybe that works in the short run, but it's not the best management plan. When faced with damage that doesn't lend itself to easy solutions or a quick fix, you must find out what caused the egg to break and the best way to fix it. Otherwise, every new egg you buy will break the same way and you won't be able to fix any of them.

The remaining chapters show you ways to repair broken eggs not only by talking about the subject but also by modeling effective problem-solving techniques.

Chapter 2

Broken Eggs at Brown, Inc.: Role Models

Diane Jones, costing supervisor, first models a poor way of handling the problems in her costing unit of a medium-size motivation and incentive travel company. She was saddled at the start with a situation that she couldn't seem to cope with; but in the end, she got the problem under control and solved it.

This story and its happy ending are fiction and some of the cast are composites of people; but the problems are real, and the situation could happen anywhere, in any organization. Although early on, Diane appears frantic and makes many mistakes, she and two of her peers, Dan Hyatt and Paula Greene, become positive role models, illustrating how to make broken eggs look as good as new.

Here's the story: Brown, Inc., a profitable company, built its solid and loyal customer base from a history of honest, quick service and exciting programs. Until recently, the company's main source of income was from small- to medium-size groups—100 to 250 people. Three years ago, senior management recognized the profitability of their less-emphasized large-group business—300 people or more—and decided to expand into those areas.

The salespeople loved it. One $600,000 contract for a group of 500 people produced more commission income than five or six contracts for smaller groups, especially since Brown, Inc., encouraged the new business by paying a higher commission rate for bigness.

Gross income jumped, but instead of a healthy 10 or 15 percent, the rate jumped to an extraordinary 38 percent in less than a year. Happy days were here again, but only for a little while.

The cost of doing business rose. Prospects, confronted with their own need for meeting deadlines, began to reject contracts before they were processed. Then long-time customers began to cancel programs because of nonperformance. The profitability of large-group business soon sagged, and the problems started to surface.

The salespeople squawked first. Delays were eroding their old customer base, and their income backed up because commissions weren't paid until the contracts are signed. No one seemed to know what was happening or how to fix it.

That was partially because no one noticed that trying to keep pace with the new business put the operations division under great pressure. Program managers (people who design and implement the final project) put in as many as fifteen hours a week in overtime, in addition to time spent running the programs. Costers (people who calculate the price of a project) stayed overtime almost as long, and word processors (people who prepare the contracts for delivery) worked almost as many hours overtime as did the costers. All these folks worked all these extra hours just to fall off of the wall, not to maintain their balance.

"Don't worry. We'll get the contracts out," was the answer the salespeople received in the beginning. Then it became, "What do you want? We're working as hard and as fast as we can."

Two years into the situation, the operations manager retired, leaving a mess for Henry Adams to clean up. However, Henry, coming from outside the company and from a much larger organization in St. Louis, had no idea that the problem even existed until several people in the costing unit stirred up a mini-revolt and quit.

The king's troops were stumped. Henry had to answer to his boss, the executive vice-president, who had to answer to his boss, the chief executive officer; and the CEO had to answer to the board of directors. Only no one had any answers, just the broken eggs.

Two months after the turmoil in the costing unit—with customers still waiting for their contracts, salespeople still squawking, and everyone tired of the whole mess—Henry silently took his place at the head of the conference table. Grim-faced, he surveyed the assembled group to see who was there and who was missing. Diane sat next to him, to his left. Dan, program management supervisor, sat opposite him. Paula, word processing supervisor, sat to Diane's left.

"Where are your senior program managers?" asked Henry.

"They're kinda busy, Henry," Dan answered.

"I asked you to have your best people here. We have serious problems to deal with."

Dan, a much older and grayer man than his boss, leaned across the table and wagged his finger. "We always handle problems ourselves. We can handle this without disrupting all of Operations."

"To date, your handling hasn't produced many results," Henry said. "We need to figure out what's wrong and what to do about it. Let's get as many brains working on this as we can."

Dan turned sideways in his chair, folded his arms across his chest, and stared at the crease where the ceiling and wall met.

"I don't know," Diane blurted out, her voice rising a half octave as she spoke. "It's really my problem. Maybe I'm missing something here, but since it's my problem, you should let me handle it myself.

"We just don't have enough people, and those we have aren't trained. You know we just lost several experienced costers. I don't know what else we can do! Give me a few more people and a few more months, and we'll get back on track."

"More people and more time," Henry reflected.

"That's all we need."

"To do what?"

Diane looked puzzled. "Maybe I'm missing something here but aren't we talking about the bottleneck in my unit?"

Henry kept his voice firm but pleasant. "No, Diane,

you're not missing anything. We *are* talking about the bottleneck, wherever it is. We're talking about its *causes*."

Dan leaned back across the table, jabbing his finger at Henry to emphasize each syllable. "Selling large groups."

"Could be. If it is, what should we do about it?"

"Stop selling them. Give us all a chance to catch up."

Paula finally spoke up, too. "My girls do whatever they can to get the contracts out the door as fast as they get the information from sales and costing. So, what's the problem?"

Diane angrily challenged her manager. "I resent you calling us in here and telling us we have to call in all our people—disrupt our units—when we don't have time for all this. We need to get back out there and finish putting together those contracts. We know what we're doing, and we can handle our problems ourselves."

Everyone was trying to speak at one time. No one had come prepared to do any serious problem solving, although Henry's memo had spelled out the agenda and the results he had hoped to get. His supervisors were too defensive to help much today. Best to go with their flow for now than try to force them to do the impossible: to think rationally.

Suppressing his urge to adjourn the meeting and haul each person into this office one at a time and fire him or her, Henry responded to each point.

"Dan, you want us to cut back on large group sales."

"No. Stop selling large groups *altogether*—for six months. Sell small groups only. We've no problems with those 'cause it doesn't take much to put one of them together and on stage."

"Paula, you say we don't have a problem."

"No, I didn't say *you, Diane,* or *Dan* don't. I said, *I* don't."

Through clenched teeth, Diane hissed at the older woman. "Then, let us solve our problems ourselves—without your snide remarks."

Henry stepped in quickly. "I don't want to dictate a solution. We've been given six months to get working up to par. So, I'll tell you what I'm going to do.

"Diane, you say it's your problem. I'm going to let you solve it. To keep us up-to-date, we'll meet every week during the crisis, or when needed. Everyone get out the work the best you can until Diane comes up with a long-term plan to solve it."

"Stop selling large groups," Dan demanded. "She can't do anything unless you stop the growth in that business."

"Okay. I'll talk with Sales. Maybe Bob can do something to help us here. But, Dan, I don't think holding back on large-group sales will solve the whole problem. The ball's in your court, Diane. You say you know what to do. Do it."

Chapter 3

The Crack in the Egg: Symptoms of Problems vs. Their Causes

Since "broken egg" is merely a metaphor for "problem," it may be a good idea to be more specific before trying to identify different kinds of problems. The *New Lexicon Webster's Dictionary of the English Language* (1987) defines a problem as:

> A question whose answer is doubtful or difficult to find; a question for discussion or consideration; a matter that causes worry or perplexity.

That definition assumes that before the question arises, something happens: a feeling or sensing that something is not right, a discomfort or uneasiness that something is wrong, needed, or wanted.

In the story, Diane sensed that something was wrong, but she did what most people do: confused symptoms with causes. Most people spot symptoms of a problem and treat them as if they were the problem itself. They spend much time and many resources pouring glue into the cracks, without identifying what caused the problem in the first place. In many cases, not only don't they have a sound plan for repairing the situation, they have no blueprint to show them what the results should look like.

It helps to have some idea—at the start—of what *should* or *could be* in order to decide if *what is* is right or not. Without a plan, the first signs of a problem usually show up as customer complaints or logjams. When you have plans to guide you, deviations from

----

Which Came First

Henry: How come the egg's broken?
Diane: It has a crack in it.

----

those plans—missed deadlines or missed production goals—sound the alarm before the complaints storm in.

Usually, problem solving begins when you feel or sense that something is not quite right in your own unit or that you're missing something you need or want—when you experience the symptoms.

In the story, Diane had reached that stage. She didn't know what was wrong, but unlike Dan (who blamed Sales) or Paula (who didn't realize she might have had a problem too), she knew something was wrong or was needed in her costing area.

Without an operational plan, a person can only intuit that something bad is happening. The discomfort starts them searching for "what's wrong," and most people then attack intuited problems with intuited solutions—e.g., "More people, more time" or "Stop selling large groups."

A new school of management philosophy—Intuitive Management—has sprung up because *sometimes* intuition *works*. In some situations, this kind of *lateral thinking* helps you to see the problem as a whole, allowing you to modify or replace the conditions that produced the problem in the first place. But most frequently, intuitions are hasty generalizations born out of jumping from sensing a problem to "doing something—*anything*—even if it's wrong."

Usually, when managers face something like a logjam, they leap from sensing the symptoms to implementing a "solution." Most commonly, they blame the line employees and push people blindly to meet deadlines or production goals. Even if they temporarily break through the bottleneck, the symptoms usually return accompanied by others. In the story, two weeks after the last meeting and still with no relief from the symptoms, Diane made a new request:

"I need to drop my unit's work measurement standards."

"Lower the standards?"

"Yes. I have too many new people. We don't have time to train 'em properly. They're making too many errors. In fact, I've caught some of 'em simply quoting directly from the rate books without building in a profit margin or anything. Checking every contract will only make the bottleneck worse."

Henry frowned as he considered what Diane wanted. "If I understand you, you're saying you can get on track by the end of our six months if you drop the standards. Let anything go out, in any condition it's in, for the salespeople and the customers to settle."

"I need just a month. Time to get the people better trained, so they can check their own work. Listen, I've loaded up the few veterans we have as much as I can. I can't ask them to do more."

"Diane, what problem are you attacking?"

"The bottleneck, of course?"

"What caused the bottleneck in the first place?"

"We don't have the luxury of sitting around looking for someone to blame," Diane snapped back. "We've got alligators biting at our tails."

Henry called on every bit of his patience. "Diane, the logjam's not the problem, and I'm not casting about to find someone to blame. I'm simply saying if we can find the cause, we can fix it once and for all."

Dan leaned across the table, wagging his finger, but before he could say his piece, Henry interjected. "We cut back sales, but new contracts still wait." Dan turned sideways in his chair, crossed his arms, and contemplated the union of ceiling and wall.

"Diane," Henry continued, "since you still want to solve the problem yourself, when we meet next week, I want to hear what you think has *caused* it and what you propose to do about it."

Chapter 4

How to Spot the Cause of a Problem

Diane knew she couldn't come to the next weekly meeting empty-handed, but she didn't know how to fill her hands with what Henry wanted. Hadn't she offered several solutions to the problem, none of which he accepted?

No, she thought resignedly to herself, Henry wasn't making an unreasonable demand; he was asking her to stop jumping for the glue pot before studying the situation. He wanted her to solve the real mystery: the *cause* of the bottleneck.

As she brooded, she remembered something she had once read: A problem's objective signs resemble a soothsayer's bones, because when you shake them and throw them to the ground, they fall into patterns; managers and soothsayers both interpret the patterns; managers part company from soothsayers *only if they have a plan* for measuring how close things are to what they should be. And Henry was complaining that Diane's department didn't have a well-defined plan.

"I may not have a well-defined plan," Diane pouted, "but I have a pretty good idea of how things should be going and what would be a best-case situation here."

It took a while, but the costing supervisor finally saw that if she calmed down and thought through her list of symptoms, she could take a more systematic approach than the one she had been using up to this point. Maybe, she pondered, by asking the journalist's questions of *who, what, why, where, when, and how*, she could come up with the kind of answers the boss was looking for.

What's happening that indicates a problem exists?

To what do the indicators point? Is something *causing* the symptoms, or is something less well-defined lurking here—for example, something *not* happening?

Although Henry was not trying to fix blame on anyone, he needed to know who was involved in the situation—at what point in the process the bottleneck was occurring and also who might break through. What did they need that they didn't have? What were they doing that they shouldn't be doing? And what should they be doing that they weren't doing?

Diane's manager wanted to know the best time to attack the breakdown (*when*), the best place to attack it (*where*), and the best way to attack it (*how*). These answers would determine if the crisis was really in Operations, or somewhere else, and whether it was worthwhile to spend any more time working on it.

The continuing worksheet, shown in Exhibits 1, 2, 3, 5, and 6, can help anyone—even Diane—to restrain him- or herself from leaping from symptoms to untested solutions and come up with answers to crucial questions regarding his or her problems. Divided into six parts, the worksheet outlines all the steps a problem solver should follow when trying to solve a complex problem, especially one that involves causal or logical connections—what are called *straight-line problems*:

1. Describe experiences that suggest that a problem exists, looking for objective indicators of the problem and analyzing them.
2. Decide whether or not to take action.
3. Analyze the data and make planning decisions.
4. Devise plans and make implementation decisions.
5. Review actions and make continuation decisions.
6. Implement alternatives if necessary.

Each section of the worksheet contains illustrations taken from the story. After reading a section, work on a situation you find difficult before returning to the text. The questions in the worksheet will help you analyze whatever situation you think poses a problem for you.

If your problem turns out to be organizational—one that involves other people—you may have to wait until you finish reading this book before you can attack the problem you're considering.

Now, a problem doesn't have to concern a situation that requires *corrective* action the way Diane's does. You can also consider how best to get something you want or need that you don't have now or look for ways to improve on what you're doing now.

However, to get full value from the worksheets shown in the exhibits, use a deviation from plan or a problem that could become a crisis. Answering the questions in the worksheets will help you uncover the real trouble and suggest several alternative solutions.

Your first task, in Part 1 (Exhibit 1) is to identify what makes you think something is wrong, needed, or wanted. What objective signs or symptoms do you experience? "I don't like what's happening" isn't answer enough. The model shows you the kinds of data you should look for.

In Part 1, you identify the deviations from plan, or how things should be. Then, by answering the questions in Part 2, you decide if you have a problem. Deviations in themselves don't become problems until you or your supervisor believe you can't live with those deviations or deficiencies.

When completing Part 2, determine whether the signs arising from your situation indicate a real problem. Then decide if it's important to do something about the situation and if such an effort is within your control. Compare your indicators with your plan. See if your signs point to serious deviations or deficiencies, and ask yourself if you can live with them. If you can't, it's time to move on to the next step (Exhibits 2–5).

Excited by what she had achieved from doing the worksheet analysis, Diane persuaded Dan and Paula to do the same analyses for their units. By the end of the day, they had compiled a complete picture of all the indicators and agreed with Diane's assessment.

> The problem's in Operations, not just in Sales. We're way off the mark in everything we think we should be able to do, and we probably will

(text continues on page 17)

Exhibit 1. Problem-solving worksheet.

Part 1: Description

Describe (1) the objective signs or symptoms you believe indicate that a problem exists, (2) what you think should be happening instead, and (3) what you think constitutes the best of all possible worlds.

1. What makes you think something is wrong, needed, or wanted? Describe what you experience. Use objective language—numbers where possible.

   Illustration

   - Eighteen repeat business contracts and seven new contracts fifteen or more days past signing deadline
   - Twenty-three repeat business contracts and nine new contracts almost thirty days old
   - Negotiated changes returned to salespeople twenty-eight days after first estimate
   - Program delays producing cancellation notices, in some cases before contracts are processed
   - Excessive number of complaints from salespeople, customers, or employees from other areas about misquotes, costing errors, and word processing errors
   - Agent commissions delayed over sixty days

2. *What should be?* Using objective language, numbers where possible, describe the business plan against which you'll compare the experiences listed above. The plan should include your most reasonable or realistic goals, objectives, or standards. If you haven't such a plan, list what you would rather see.

   Illustration

   - All contracts returned to salespeople within fifteen days of receipt in office

(continued)

Exhibit 1. (*continued*)

- Negotiated changes returned to salespeople within twenty-five days after first estimate
- Misquotes or other errors of no more than 5–10 percent
- No more than one–two customer complaints a month
- At least 80 percent of old business to repeat
- No more than 10 percent rejections of terms

3. *What could be?* Using objective language, numbers where possible, describe the ideals (best cases) in the business plan, against which you'll compare the experiences listed in items 1 and 2. If you have no best-case plan, you may want to create one.

   Illustration

   - All contracts returned to salespeople within seven days of receipt in office
   - Negotiated changes returned to salespeople within twenty days after first estimate
   - Misquotes or other errors of no more than 1–2 percent
   - No more than one customer complaint a month
   - At least 90 percent old business
   - No more than 5 percent rejection of terms

Part 2: Make a Decision

Do you have a problem? Should you and can you do anything about it?

1. What would happen if you don't do anything? Describe the scenario and consequences.

   Illustration

   - The logjam will continue unabated. We'll lose our customer base and many employees, as well as a large amount of gross income.

2. Why do something about it? Describe the scenario and consequences.

Illustration

- Business objective: Generate a profit for our investors. Corrective action will maintain and develop more profitable large-group business.

3. Who would be affected or care if you don't do anything?

   Illustration

   - All constituencies

4. Do the differences between your plan or wishes and your experience constitute a problem, or can you live with the differences?

   Illustration

   - Far-reaching and long-term corrective action needed immediately

5. Is corrective action within your control?

   Illustration

   - We can take the necessary steps to bring corrective action into our control by collaborating with Sales and the other operational departments.

---

continue to miss no matter what we do. For some reason, we're not prepared to handle any significant growth, period. The way things are, unless we take a closer look at how we do things, we may never catch up.

Their analyses led to the conclusion that a real problem existed, and showed where it existed. Regardless of Sales, they had a problem all their own, entitled How We Do Things.

Taking a Closer Look

"So, you've persuaded us of the obvious," Paula chided. "We have a problem. You have any ideas on how to solve it?"

Diane's elation flattened. "My plan won't sunset at the end of the month, like I said. We're still too far behind. I think we need to accelerate the plan. Check even fewer contracts. Run them all out to your people, Paula, to enter and process as fast as we can."

Paula's eyes narrowed, and she pursed her lips as she considered the suggestion. "You're pushing my girls to the max. What do you think this bright idea will do to 'em? How do you think they feel when they see all those contracts coming down the pike—especially since they'll know they're full of errors?

"Your plan's a boa constrictor that swallows a pig whole. You can see the lump passing down the length of the snake, and you know what comes out the other end!"

"Everyone's upset over the poor quality of the work as it is," Dan contributed. "Henry wants cause, not effect. We've done nothing more here than clearly state effects that show we're in trouble. Paula's right. We're beating on the obvious."

Instead of intimidating her, Paula's and Dan's remarks challenged Diane to push on. "Well, if the signs are so obvious, why shouldn't their causes be also? I, for one, feel we're finally getting somewhere. It's my fault we haven't, because I've been unwilling to take the necessary risks—look beyond the bottleneck itself."

Diane's excitement glowed in her eyes. "I think we've—I've—been asking the wrong questions. Now, when the questions we ask dig into the heart of the problem, I'm ready to ask new ones—like, Is there a new way to do it? Do we need more of the same really, or do we need to give what we do a new twist? Maybe we need less of the same? I don't know yet, but I'm willing to take a fresh look at things."

"It'll take forever," Paula complained.

"I don't think so, not if we look at how other people do the same sorts of things. Maybe we can borrow or adapt methods. Substitute other methods for what we're doing, procedures that have been tried and tested."

Dan caught a little of Diane's excitement and joined in. "Y'know. I've been thinking. Since we put all this stuff together—if we look at the whole picture here, maybe we can rearrange parts of the organization and parts of the workflow. Maybe combine things." He laughed, "Blow Henry's mind. Do everything just the opposite of what we do now."

"That would shake him up," Diane agreed. "Listen. I have to get back to my unit, and I suppose you two have a ton of work to do also, so what do you say we burn some midnight oil? Have a pizza sent in for dinner—my treat—and kick this around for a few hours? Can you stay late?"

"Wait a minute, lady," Paula snapped. "You said it yourself. It's your problem."

"I don't think so anymore. We're all in it together."

"I have to admit she's right," Dan agreed.

Paula grudgingly agreed too. "Yes, I admit it, but I don't know what to do about it. Diane, you have to figure this out, not us."

Surprised at Paula's resistance, Diane stammered a bit as she struggled for support. "Th-the logjam seems to belong to all of us. It's, uh— Moving the contracts out of costing as fast as they come in, as you said, only dumps them on your unit. That means we *all* get more people and more time, or we continue with my plan, or we come up with something more effective."

Paula sighed audibly. "All right. I'll call home. I guess one thing's for sure. Until we identify the real problem, we won't solve it. I still think it's only *your* problem. The logjam's in your area, but it's sure affecting everyone else."

"I guess that makes it an organizational-centered problem, like Henry says, and it may have its roots in several areas. We've got some tough questions to answer."

Both Paula and Dan checked with their families and discovered no urgent reasons for leaving the office on time. They stayed, although no one knew quite what they were going to do.

Chapter 5

What Kind of Problem Do You Face?

The supervisors are now on a roll *because* they're asking the right questions. They've cut through the symptoms to their roots, and now they're planning to cut through the roots as well. New ways of looking at situations, such as Diane and Dan are suggesting, lay the foundation for genuinely creative problem solving. But first, they have to settle some basic issues: What kind of problems are they trying to solve—individual or organizational, analytic or diffuse?

Self-Centered Problem Solving

Individuals have or create certain problems that don't lend themselves well to group problem solving. Diane first thought she had that kind of problem. Consulting with other people only to pick their brains, she thought she had what is called a *self-centered problem,* i.e., a problem that belonged to her alone.

 When the problem or its solution revolves around you, you're obviously the center. Personal problems, situations with which only you should deal because of some special knowledge or authority you have, belong to you. They are self-centered, as distinguished from organizational-centered, problems. That Diane's situation didn't meet the five criteria of a self-centered problem, as shown in the sidebar, made it clear that she'd been looking at her Humpty Dumpty through a narrow glass.

 Consider responsibility first. The problem is self-

----

centered if it's your responsibility to work alone on solving it. Either the demand is built into your job, or you've been ordered to work by yourself.

If only you can make the decisions necessary to solve the problem, you have no choice but to solve it by yourself. Apart from being *ordered* to work alone, you may have to work alone for another reason: Only you have the knowledge or the ability to solve the problem.

In a highly technical job—a specialized one in electronics or space technology, for example—only a select few have the knowledge or the skill to understand and deal with symptoms, let alone discover the causes. You must work alone under those circumstances.

But Diane is a costing supervisor, not an atomic scientist. Other people have the knowledge and skills for her to call upon to help solve the problem.

Time constraints don't bother her either. If Henry had ordered, "I want answers *now*," that would have been different. Immediate answers demand quick decisions that a group process can't supply. Although seeking consensus usually produces better or more effective results than solo flying, it takes time to pull a group together, assign roles, develop ideas, and test them. So if time is a luxury, you'd better make decisions for yourself.

Nor do personal problems belong in the public domain. One-to-one with a supervisor if it's a performance problem and one-to-one with a counselor if it's an emotional or behavior crisis are all the public airing such unpleasantness should get. In fact, pressing your peers or other coworkers for help on private matters can be disruptive and counterproductive.

The explanation of a self-centered problem doesn't describe Diane's situation as a whole. When a problem is self-centered, you take responsibility for working it out by yourself.

Now, while the whole situation seems to belong to the group in the story, one part of it definitely can be solved only by Diane. Why? Because she's one of many people who suffer from computerphobia. After taking a look at what makes the problem in the story a group problem, I'll talk about what Diane can do gain control over her personal one too.

Organizational-Centered Problems

When a problem is organizational-centered, you share responsibility for dealing with it with other people. From what's been said so far, it seems that Diane was right to turn to the other supervisors for help.

Volumes of studies show that two or more heads are better than one, especially if more than one head should be involved. In the absence of the constraints tied to self-centered problems, a group, properly facilitated, frequently produces more effective results than any one person can. All the same, certain conditions should prevail before you call in the troops.

You need to have some time to spare. As I said earlier, calling on the group, assigning roles, giving each person sufficient background, and permitting the members the opportunity to work on the problem take time. How much time depends on your circumstances. In Diane's case, time was not a major factor—yet.

If the problem originates somewhere within the organization or has something to do with the way it operates or does business, calling on members of the

----

Organizational-Centered Problems
Criteria

1. Time permits the group to work on it.
2. The problem has its origins within the organization or some process inside it.
3. The knowledge or skill is present in the group or can be acquired in a reasonable amount of time.
4. Group problem solving has been mandated.
5. The comfort level of the group is high enough to permit it.

----

organization makes sense. The problem belongs to the group, not to you, so let the group solve it.

Besides, the knowledge and skill needed to solve an organizational-centered problem usually can be found in the group. Sometimes, even if you have what it takes to get the job done by yourself, it's to your advantage—time permitting—to let other people acquire the information or the skill. It gives them a stake in the solution and generates a commitment to see the solution through. Nothing motivates as well as a challenge.

For more discussion of the advantages of delegating problems to other people, see another book in the Successful Office Skills series, *How to Delegate Effectively.*

Of course, if you've been told, "Get the unit behind this," your mandate governs your response. Call in the troops. But be careful! Your group may not be ready for participatory management.

Many employees have had little opportunity to join in a genuine group effort. They are not used to it and, not trusting the motive behind the request, tend to be suspicious of supervisors who ask for their help: "What's the matter? Can't handle the responsibility? Want to spread the blame around if things don't work out?" Be sure the group's comfort level meets the level of the challenge.

Giving the Troops a Chance

People accustomed to taking orders rarely do well at governing themselves or solving their own problems. Without the king's direction, the troops are helpless. That's why so many people believe the old saying: "A camel is a horse designed by a committee." And that's probably true if the committee is poorly run.

If study after study and experience after experience show that a group attack on complex problems works well, how can we give the king's troops a fair chance?

We can answer that question best by comparing how a dictatorial king's troops would go about trying to fix up old Humpty with what happens in a successful problem-solving group such as a work unit, committee, or task force. But unless the conditions listed in the sidebar characterize the way the group goes about its business, expect it to fail.

First, without a mandate to *do* the job, a problem-solving group won't function effectively. In a world ruled by a dictator, why would the troops take responsibility for putting Humpty Dumpty together again? It's the king's problem, not theirs.

A successful group has the authority as well as the responsibility to solve its problems *and* implement the solutions it comes up with. In the absence of a dictator's veto power, the members of the group can do what they've been asked to do and each person has a personal stake in the group's success or failure. Instead of no one taking responsibility, everyone does.

Successful Groups

1. Have the authority as well as responsibility to implement decisions.
2. Provide input and feedback.
3. Multiply creative energy; create synergy.
4. Balance task and process.
5. Decide by consensus rather than by majority rule.
6. Share the recognition.

Second, a complex problem is hard to decipher without a sufficient amount of information. Poorly functioning groups suffer from leadership that inhibits or does not encourage the free exchange of information. Poor leadership allows individuals to inadvertently or deliberately withhold data the group needs. Often, a dictator in the workplace amasses the wealth (information) for personal gain. In that case, the group as a whole is worse off than an individual working alone.

When people share responsibility, they increase the avenues through which information and feedback flow. Instead of only the dictator amassing all the wealth, each person contributes his or her knowledge or skills to the *group*. The group then multiplies each person's abilities, whereas individuals operating alone or out of sync with the group rely on themselves only. What tyrant doesn't know how lonely it is at the top?

Third, look at how limited the energy of one person or a divided group is. A divided group *wastes* its energy on bickering or game playing—in nonproductive work.

Not only does a successful group multiply its resources, it also multiplies its energy. An effective leader understands the "magic" of a successful group: synergy.

Originally a medical concept, "synergy" means the working together of two or more muscles. During the past twenty years or so, the idea has been linked more closely to the concepts of synthesizing and energy: focusing the energy of a group on a common goal.

To synthesize means to form different elements into one whole. Energy means, in one sense, a forcefulness or vigor or vitality and, in another sense, the unifying concept of physical science—that which draws all systems of matter together into one whole. Forming individuals into one whole and focusing it on a common goal generates an energy analogous to the energy of an atom; its output is greater than the sum of its parts. No king can overlook this energy and remain long on the throne.

To separate dictators from leaders, watch them in action. How the person at the head of the table uses his or her position—to benefit him- or herself or to benefit the group—determines whether or not the group succeeds. Fourth in a successful group leaders facilitate problem solving to meet the group's needs, and their effectiveness determines the group's effectiveness. Since despots command solutions to meet their own needs, their troops make camels out of horses.

And, so, we come to the fifth condition that characterizes a successful group. Unless the group maintains a balance in its sense of what it's doing, it loses direction and fails. Only if the leader facilitates rather than dominates can he or she maintain a balance between the two different orientations that mark a group process: task orientation and process orientation.

Since success means coming up with a workable answer to the question at hand, the group must focus on tasks. It has to get results; otherwise it can't achieve its problem-solving mission.

Unenlightened kings err on the side of that orientation: They go for results, the bottom line. Task orientation concentrates on *what* people do without also caring about *how* they do it. It generates bickering, power struggles, inefficiencies, and ineffective outcomes. Frequently, instead of solving problems, the group creates new ones.

Enlightened leaders understand that how people feel about what they do, what they feel about themselves and about the group, affects what they do. By managing the group members' interaction with each other, the facilitator sees to it that each member makes a contribution appropriate to his or her needs, wishes, or abilities and is recognized for it. That way, no one feels run over, used, or abused.

The sixth characteristic of a successful problem-solving group prevents those feelings. In camel-producing groups, most people feel run over, used, or abused. They feel that the king or the king's lackeys make all the decisions for them, the troops, to carry out.

Leaders of successful groups use the decision-making process itself to ensure that no one feels oppressed by the group or by any one individual. They see to it that all participates in whatever way they can. That way, each person feels the decisions belong to him or her.

The leader also prevents a norm of "group think," in which everyone thinks as one mind, usually the head person's. Some enlightened leaders use majority rule, which is okay at times, but it commonly results in a tyranny of the greatest number.

To avoid majority rule or group think, effective leaders encourage disagreement or differences of opinions. They then facilitate consensus taking, which I'll discuss in more detail later. At this time, it's sufficient to say only that a leader uses consensus to allow the group to reach agreement about alternative solutions to the problems.

When leaders allow disagreements or differences of opinion and seek consensus, they don't give up control; unless the group operates under reasonable controls, it can't function.

The seventh characteristic of a successful problem-solving group requires a leader to control how the group functions, but he or she exercises control through mutual respect. Rather than push or pull the members along, an effective leader creates a climate in which creativity and creative problem solving are simply norms, not sometime things.

That climate comes about, in part, by sharing the honors as well as the blame with the group. A leader only represents the group, and since no one person bears the burden of being expected to do what perhaps the group itself can't, the payoff as well as the effort is shared.

To prevent failure, or to prevent finger-pointing if the group does fail, everyone collaborates and cooperates with one another. The sense of the group is that "we're all in this together, sink or swim. The only way to succeed is to share both the pain and the glory."

So much for the two kinds of problems. When you get to Exhibit 2, you'll have an opportunity to decide whether your own problem is self-centered or organizational-centered. For now, let's look at two other types of problems: analytic and diffuse.

Chapter 6

How to Approach Analytic and Diffuse Problems

Analytic problems, whether they are self-centered or organizational-centered, are also either *straight-line* or *vertical problems*. These situations almost always involve causal or logical connections in which you can see that if A happens, B will happen, too, or if Statement A is true, then so is statement B. The popular Left-Brain/Right-Brain theory says that "left-brain thinking," such as you find among mathematicians or those using the scientific method, works best for solving these problems.

On the other hand, diffuse problems, which also can be either self-centered or organizational-centered, involve values, meanings, and attitudes—conditions that affect the way things are done or the relationships between people but that are not clearly identifiable through ordinary analysis. The same popular theory says that "right-brain thinking," such as what you find among artists and poets, works best for solving these problems.

It's not that right- and left-brain thinking can't work together to solve problems. Rather, you can apply either type of thinking to any kind of problem, or you can apply what's called whole-brain thinking to any situation, as I will when I discuss brainstorming.

I separate analytic from diffuse problems at this time only to point out their differences. It'll be easier to understand them this way.

Analytic and Diffuse Problems

Analytic Problems: Straight-line or vertical; left-brain thinking applies. Well-defined, clear and unambiguous parts, most frequently connected by cause and effect or logic. The problem occurs when something goes wrong with the connections between the parts.

Diffuse Problems: Mainly poorly-defined; holistic; right-brain thinking controls. Usually involves values, attitudes, perceptions, assumptions, and the problem doesn't lend itself to "standardized" ways of seeing things or thinking. Often surfaces as a feeling that something can be better.

Analytic Problems

In a straight-line problem, the situation is well-defined. All the parts are clear. There is little ambiguity. And the factors involved are connected most frequently by cause and effect or by logic. A problem surfaces when you sense that something has gone wrong with the connections. For example, Brown's managers expected increased income from large-group sales to increase profits—a straight-line connection, right? Yes. But that connection passed through several other points in the process between income and profits, and somewhere along the way, something interfered with the connection between income and profit.

Usually when you say you're going to solve an analytic problem, you mean you're going to "fix" the broken connection; you're going to use analytic tools, such as statistical or financial analysis. You're going to restore the connections through logical adjustments to the process. However, sometimes, because cause and effect or logical implications aren't evident, straight-line thinking doesn't work. When it doesn't, you need to apply "lateral" thinking, which some theorists (e.g., Edward de Bono) call the only truly creative thinking.

Diffuse Problems

Lateral thinking isn't straight-line. You don't look for cause and effect or logical connections. In fact, diffuse problems—whether self-centered or organizational-centered—don't always begin with discomfort or a feeling that something is wrong. Instead, although they may involve vertical elements, they are, in the main, poorly defined and holistic. That's why problems often surface through a feeling that although everything seems okay, something can be better. They provide an opportunity, a challenge.

Since diffuse problems usually involve values, attitudes, perceptions, assumptions, or meanings and not events, things, or logic, they don't lend themselves well to "standardized" ways of seeing things or thinking. For example, a diffuse problem may *cause* an interpersonal conflict between two managers, but the root problem, e.g., a values conflict, is not amenable to analytic techniques; so you use lateral thinking to resolve the issue.

When you think laterally, you reorganize information and assumptions about the situation you're considering. Since you're not dealing with logical, chronological, or causal connections, you have to become illogical in your thinking and question assumptions and customary ways of thinking or doing things.

Thinking artistically rather than scientifically or mathematically helps. Looking at the whole picture first and then taking it apart and viewing parts in new and different ways characterize right-brain thinking, because the right side of the brain controls diffuse rather than analytic problem solving.

That's what Diane and Dan were doing when we last saw them. They were challenging their situation and its assumptions with some tough questions:

- Can we do things in a new way?
- Can we substitute something else for what we're doing?
- Can we borrow from or adapt what other people do?
- Can we give old ways a new twist?

- Do we merely need more of the same?
- Maybe, we need less of the same?
- Can we rearrange what we're already doing?
- Can we do everything in reverse?
- Can we combine methods or functions?

So, if logic doesn't work and you need to apply creative, lateral thinking such as intuition or visual imagery, then you need to take a closer look at creativity because one person's creativity is often another person's insanity. What is creativity or creative thinking? Let's ask Mr. Webster to help out.

> *"creativity": n* ability to create
> *"to create": vt* to bring into being; to invest with a new form; to make something happen, cause, make; to produce through imagination; design; **syn** see INVENT
> *"thinking": n* the mental process

I can now produce my own definition of *creative thinking.*

> Using one's mind to bring new thoughts into being; to invest with one's mind a new form; to make something new happen by a course of action originating in one's mind; to cause something new to happen, to make something new; to produce new ideas through imagination; to design something new; to invent something new.

Notice the number of times the word "new" comes up in that definition? That's what creativity and creative thinking are all about: newness. Too many times a person's eggs lie shattered forever because he or she honestly believes the old adage "There's nothing new under the sun."

Many different glues can repair diffuse problems. Look at all the new words: "brainstorming," "synectics," "force fit ideas," "forced relationships," "lists," "visualization," "morphological analysis," "lateral thinking," "divergent thinking," "convergent thinking."

Don't worry, this little book doesn't have the space to discuss them all, and I'll save my discussion of brainstorming and lateral thinking for when you finish identifying the shape and complexion of your own broken eggs.

The Brown, Inc., case study clearly shows an organizational-centered and analytic problem, although the fact that some costers (including Diane) and program managers were reluctant to use their PCs raised the possibility of at least one diffuse situation: a fear of technology or a reluctance to give up old ways of doing things. Whichever it was, values and attitudes were involved. Just what was involved can be uncovered in Part 3 (Exhibit 2).

Now, go on to Exhibit 2 and read Part 3 of the continuing worksheet. Analyze the indicators themselves. Ask and answer the *when, who,* and *where* questions, which will give you the answers to "What kind of problem do I have: self-centered or organizational-centered, analytic or diffuse?"

Exhibit 2. Part 3: Analysis of the indicators and making planning decisions

A. *Analyze the Indicators:* Obtain as comprehensive a picture from the data as you can by answering these questions:

1. *"When" Questions.* When did the indicators begin showing up? Under what circumstances? When do they reach their peak? How often do they occur? When do they occur most frequently? When do they occur least frequently? Use historical data going back as far as possible. [*I summarize information. Be more specific and detailed in your analysis.*]

   Illustration

   • The indicators first showed up three years ago, after growth in large-group business exceeded 9.5 percent.

- They are at their highest level when growth exceeds 38 percent and increase rapidly every time growth exceeds 15 percent.
- They diminish only when growth decreases to under 9 percent.

2. *"Who" Questions.* (1) Who's involved prior to the appearance of the indicators? (2) Who's involved during the appearance of the indicators? (3) Who's affected by the indicators?

   Illustration

   - Item 1: The salespeople, accounts receivable.
   - Item 2: The program managers, the costing, data processing.
   - Item 3: The word processors, the agents, customers.

3. *"Where" Questions.* Where do the indicators show up most frequently? Least frequently?

   Illustration

   - Most frequently in costing and word processing.
   - Least frequently in accounts receivable.

4. *Mixed Questions.* What equipment and materials are involved (available, needed)? Who's using them? Who's not? What or who's missing and should be there?

   Illustration

   - Mainframe and CRTs, PCs, calculators, pricing manuals, printers, folders, sorters.
   - Accounts receivable (mainframe and CRTs); all program managers—but some are not using their PCs; all costers, but some are not using their CRT's.

(continued)

Exhibit 2. (*continued*)

- Accounts receivable processing equipment most complete; not all program managers are using CRTs or PCs; only one coster adept at the PC or CRT.

B. *Planning Decisions:* Decide on the types of problems with which you're confronted—self-centered or organizational, analytic or diffuse—and who should be involved.

   1. Self-centered or organizational problem? Explain.

      Illustration

      - Organizational problem. Equipment, training needed in program management, costing. Gaps in workflow.

   2. Analytic or Diffuse Problem? Explain.

      Illustration

      - Analytic problem, tied to gaps in equipment, training, and workflow management. Underuse of PCs may be a diffuse problem.

   3. How should you proceed? Identify the steps you think you should take for *working* on the problem—*not* to be construed as a solution to the problem itself.

      Illustration

      a. Create task force; analyze organizational problems; make recommendations to executive committee for long-range crisis management plan.
      b. Create work group of employees and supervisors for short-term emergency plan.

c. Meet with the work group immediately; outline indicators; charge it with responsibility and limited authority.
d. Set deadline for emergency plan.
e. Meet with task force after work group; outline indicators; charge it with responsibility and limited authority subject to approval from executive management. May involve some of the same people, plus people from connected areas.
f. Set deadline.

Chapter 7

Problem-Solving Methods That Work

Although the Brown, Inc., case study emphasizes the large problem—ending the bottleneck permanently—Diane has been wrestling with a smaller but critical part of it: identifying the real problem that causes the bottleneck. Uncover the real problem and the solution usually jumps out at you—as if by intuitive insight. Let's see how the supervisors handled this phase of the problem-solving process.

The pizza arrived just at the close of the business day.

"I think better on a full stomach," Diane explained. "And, it'll give us time to read some materials Henry sent us after I told him we were meeting tonight. I think it's the first time he's smiled when we talked about this situation."

"Pleased?" Paula asked.

"I'd say so. I glanced through the article on brainstorming he wants us to read. It'll help us work through the questions he had his secretary type up for us. I thought we could read them while we eat dinner."

"This stuff's sure to give me gas," Dan groused after flipping through the article and then the worksheets. "Why do we have to read this and go through all these questions? I still say, Cut out sales for several months and the problem'll go away on its own."

Diane shook her head. "The boss doesn't agree, and after we three talked it over this afternoon, I don't agree anymore, either. As for all these questions, I asked him the same thing. What for? You'll never guess his answer."

"No, I won't, so tell us," Dan responded.

"He asked another question. 'How do you eat an elephant?' "

"Now, what's that supposed to mean?"

"Well, how would you?"

Paula turned up her nose. "Who'd *want* to eat an elephant?"

"If you did have to eat one, how would you do it?"

"Cut out the riddles," Dan complained. "What's the answer?"

"One bite at a time."

"Okay. I *still* don't get it."

"Dan, can't you see? It's a big, tough problem, involving a whole lot of parts. A simple problem calls for simple methods. A big one like this means we have to deal with its little pieces one at a time instead of continuing to attack 'the bottleneck.' We're trying to eat the whole elephant in one giant gulp. C'mon. Let's eat the pizza instead."

"Well, maybe this brainstorming stuff *can* help us, but I still think. . . ."

"We all know what you think," Paula interrupted. "Now, stop it before you strain yourself. Read!"

So what *is* this "brainstorming stuff"? As well-known as it is, it's surprising that it's so poorly implemented most of the time.

Brainstorming, devised in 1938 by Alex Osborn, and two other approaches to problem identification—divergent and convergent thinking—appear to overlap in style and form. They give free rein to your imagination while using either lateral (right-brain) thinking to get a feel for the whole problem or straight-line (left-brain) thinking to cut through an analytic problem. In brainstorming, you allow any type of creative thinking to apply itself to the problem, but in a controlled and systematic way.

Divergent Thinking

Through divergent thinking, you think about the problem in as many different ways as you can without trying to solve it. You just try to get some idea of what it is.

The method can be described as hypothetical trial and error.

Study the symptoms. Hypothetically connect those symptoms to each other in such a way as to see the whole picture at once. In the process of putting the parts together—putting the pieces together as you would put together a jigsaw puzzle for which you have no picture to follow—you should be able to define your problem, especially a diffuse one.

Instead of taking the whole situation apart, you look for the breakdown by taking in as much of it as possible—much like an artist looking at a blank canvas and mentally filling it with an image. The meanings involved in the situation, or the causal connections that have become disconnected, emerge from the picture. In the process of defining the problem, you are likely to see or intuit its solution.

Practice this technique by using the list of indicators in Part 1 of the worksheet, shown in Exhibit 1 and trying to define the problem at Brown, Inc. Or use your own list of indicators if you have already listed them all.

Convergent Thinking

Through convergent thinking, you take an approach opposite to that in divergent thinking: You eat the elephant one bite at a time.

When using convergent thinking, you are sometimes able to solve a problem by solving some part of it. First, you cut the problem into the smallest pieces you can. Then you study each part and exercise your best judgment to decide which one seems important enough to work on.

For example, Diane might ask herself and her costers to look at their concerns about using the PC. They could list them and attack the one they think is the most important inhibitor. If they then worked on that one concern, they could, in the process, push past the others.

Other times, you solve a problem, especially a diffuse one, by connecting the parts in unique ways.

Since it's difficult to illustrate how to make "unique connections," I'll ask you to think of the process this way:

Hypothetical thinking allows you to look at a "what-if" world, one that doesn't exist but could if you set your mind and resources to bringing it about. As a result, although events in a what-if world may be improbable, they are all possible. Convergent thinking releases you from reality—at least for the moment—and allows you to imagine whatever you want.

Early in the brainstorming process, which I'll describe next, it pays to use convergent thinking as the way to approach the process of considering all possible ideas for either identifying or solving the problem at hand. Since, in convergent thinking or in the uncritical phase of brainstorming, you don't analyze or criticize ideas when you're generating them, no idea is too far out to consider. Many an off-the-wall idea has become a successful, money-making product.

Brainstorming

While divergent and convergent thinking tend to be right-brain methods for attacking problems, brainstorming integrates both right- and left-brain patterns of thinking by permitting any and all ideas to surface during the uncritical phase of the process. Now, while this technique works best when applied to organizational-centered problems, nothing prevents an individual working alone from brainstorming by him- or herself. All you need is paper or a chalkboard on which to write.

If yours is a self-centered problem, on your own, follow the process I apply to solving organizational problems. On the paper or chalkboard, uncritically and nonjudgmentally list all your ideas with respect to what could be causing the problem or what the problem could be. Don't think about the ideas; instead, freely associate as you would in convergent thinking. Only after you've exhausted all possibilities should you examine what you've written. As I said, the process doesn't differ from what follows with regard to solving organizational-centered problems.

In its ideal form, brainstorming is a structured, facilitated activity in which a group meets at a specified time. Group members appear with a previously published agenda and ideas in hand. During the meeting, they follow procedures set up by someone not actively engaged in the process. Although the facilitator may be a member of the group, it's better to bring in an uninvolved person. The group leader should avoid the facilitator role in order to ensure full participation and to prevent group think.

After the group leader (not the facilitator) repeats and explains the purpose of the agenda and answers questions, he or she turns the meeting over to the facilitator. Ideally, this would be a person from a work area having no vested interest in the results—for example, someone from human resources.

The facilitator then sets the ground rules, which are listed in the sidebar.

The Brown, Inc., case illustrates something less than the ideal, because, in most cases, people work in a setting similar to this. Most ordinary work groups don't have the luxury of a neutral party playing the role of facilitator. Larger organizations can provide one, but smaller groups usually can't. As in our case, someone from the group usually backs out of actively entering into the discussion unless someone else takes up the marker, pencil, or chalk and lets him or her play an active role.

Brainstorming
Ground Rules

1. Generate ideas without interruption until the group runs dry.
2. Don't stop to evaluate, analyze, or criticize until the group says it's ready.
3. Analyze the ideas.
4. Select the alternative solution for testing by consensus.

The facilitator describes the situation to be examined, as he or she understands it. This sets the stage for the discussion.

Generating Ideas

In the scenario, Paula wore the facilitator's hat first, because she still thought the problem belonged to Dan and Diane, not to her. Instead of describing the situation, she read Henry's questions and allowed the others to fire at her any idea that come to mind. No idea was too extreme or off-the-wall:

"Okay. The first question: When did the situation first surface?"

"When the lid came off large-group sales," Dan shouted.

"When salespeople and customers started complaining about delays getting out the contracts," Diane called out.

"That's crazy!" Dan countered. The angry looks the women gave him sat him back in his chair, hands over his mouth.

"It must have been, oh, two years ago," Diane continued.

"Three!" Dan offered.

"When errors cropped up in all the spot checks, and. . . ."

We don't need to include all their answers. You get the idea. Generate the ideas non-stop without evaluating, analyzing, or criticizing anything until someone says, as Dan did, "Enough already."

"Do you agree, Di?"

"Yes, I think we've beaten that question to death."

Analysis

When you analyze the ideas generated, look for repetitions and redundancies first. Then look for the connections between ideas. Connecting ideas helps weed out irrelevant items because irrelevancies tend to stand alone.

Later in the evening, with Paula and Diane brain-

storming and Dan facilitating, the women were beginning to analyze their answers to another question when
Diane suggested, "I think we should take out the
phrase 'analyze entry.' There, at the top of the flip
chart. It means the same and is part of what we say
later, about two thirds of the way down: 'examine all
the positions in word processing.' "

"You know," Paula began, "I think we're putting too
much emphasis on word processing here. All the different positions in word processing seem to connect
more logically with each other than they do with costing
and program management."

"What are you suggesting?"

"Add it to our list for further study. What do you
think?"

"I don't know," Diane hesitated. "The way I see it,
the costers have to work closely with the program
managers. Not so the word processing people. They
seem to work more closely with Sales than anyone
else."

Paula shook her head impatiently. "I haven't suggested that we do anything yet, really. Dan, take off
the facilitator's hat and give us your opinion."

"I think Paula has a point. I understand her to mean
that we should add analyzing those jobs to further
study, that's all."

"Oh," Diane apologized. "I guess I jumped too far
ahead—like I usually do. Sure, put that way, it makes
good sense. I agree we should add that to the list."

First, the supervisors removed a repetition. Then,
the two women analyzed an idea and disagreed on it.
Asking Dan to change roles and reenter the discussion
helped Diane see that she was arguing the wrong
point. That enabled the three of them to reach a
consensus about what to include in the items for
further study. Reaching consensus is the third part of
brainstorming.

Consensus

Reaching consensus and calling for a vote have nothing in common. Voting generates winners and losers.
Consensus taking generates only winners.

Let's dispel a myth about reaching consensus, the myth that *everyone* has to agree that an idea or a suggestion or a plan is *the* correct answer to a question. You often hear facilitators ask, "Are we all agreed on this plan?" The more accurate way of asking is, "Are we all agreed to try this plan first and, if it doesn't work, trot out one of the alternatives?"

In reaching agreement, you don't all have to agree that any answer is the only answer. Instead, since you must implement some plan to correct a bad situation, consensus allows you to implement the one that seems most beneficial at the moment.

You reach consensus by following as many of these six steps as is necessary:

1. Flying trial balloons
2. Presenting your case
3. Resolving disagreements
4. Working through a decision matrix
5. Prioritizing the alternatives
6. Making a decision

Your situation determines which steps to leave out.

I'll let the scenario show you the process of reaching consensus around a simple decision that illustrates materials in Exhibit 2: devising plans and making implementation decisions. But first, read Exhibit 3, in which the three supervisors identify alternative plans. Then, continue reading to see how the supervisors achieve the final objective of this activity: selecting a plan.

Achieving Consensus

Studying a chart doesn't help you understand much about how people use it to arrive at an agreement to do something, i.e., achieving consensus. So, let's go back to the discussion that "dark and stormy" night at Brown, Inc. At various points in the story, narrative is used to point out what's happening in the dialogue that fits with the steps of achieving consensus.

I have compressed the discussion to fit space constraints, so keep in mind that any attempt at reaching

43

Exhibit 3. Part 4: Devising and choosing alternative plans.

What are the alternatives for solving the problem? Include the substantive details, the costs of implementation, and the costs of not implementing. [*The sample summarizes the more extensive planning process that would have taken place if I had carried it through in the text.*]

Illustration

Work Group's Emergency Plans

- *Plan 1:* Now in place. Most quality controls in costing stopped. Check one in six contracts. Five percent increase in productivity to date. No extra dollar expense. Reduction in production cost negligible. Intangible cost serious.
- *Plan 2:* Augment Plan 1; stop quality controls in word processing. Bottleneck created by Plan 1. Stop checks in both areas. Projected increase in productivity, 25 percent. No extra dollar expense. Reduction in production cost negligible. Intangible cost serious.
- *Plan 3:* Continue Plan 1; fully automate costing procedures. Require all costers and program managers to work on computers or CRTs. Train costers on PCs. Production costs increased in short run by slowdown during training. Lift Plan 1 in thirty days and return to normal. Training and equipment cost estimate: $17,500. Productivity increase estimate: 40 percent after training. Intangible benefits: improvement in customer satisfaction, relations with salespeople, and employee morale.

consensus could take much longer than this and you could encounter many disagreements along the way. Remember, group problem solving takes time.

As facilitator, Dan is flying the first *trial balloon*. The three supervisors have just finished outlining three emergency plans: Diane's current plan (Plan 1), her second plan (Plan 2), and Dan's plan (Plan 3). They now have to decide which one they'll support in their report to Henry. "It seems to me" Dan said, "that we have pretty well outlined the three main emergency plans. Are we ready to decide on which one to recommend to Henry?"

"Maybe I'm missing something here," Diane responded, "but I think Plans 1 and 2 are the ony viable options right now."

Paula frowned. "I thought we'd been through this already, Di, but go ahead, make your case."

"We'd have to make too many changes if we adopted Dan's plan. People, methods, equipment. I don't think the people can handle that many changes on top of all those we've made already. Both of the other plans have the beauty of simplicity.

"And, both of them will cost a whole lot less. Dan's plan calls for training and equipment costs. Henry'll never buy it, and even if he does, executive management won't. No, I don't think that anyone will buy into Plan 3."

Paula listened impatiently, and at the first opportunity, she jumped in. "Well, if you're finished, I'd like to *make my case* for Plan 3. Dan? Does this fit with the ground rules Bruce supplied?"

"Sure."

"How do you feel about it, Diane?"

"Shoot."

"I agree that Plan 3 presents a funding problem that neither of the other two plans has; but I think the *costs* hidden in them far exceed Plan 3's expenses." Paula presented her lengthy counterpoint to Diane's suggestion, ending with "I can go on and on."

"Spare us, please," Diane protested. "But how do we justify an unbudgeted outlay? We're talking $17,500! Where do we find it?"

"Contingency funds. They're in the corporation's budget."

"I don't think they'll buy it upstairs."

Paula and Diane sat silently studying their notes. Dan waited a few seconds before running up another trial balloon. "Ready? Have we reached a consensus?"

"No. I'm not satisifed yet," Diane answered.

Feeling frustrated, Paula snapped. "Di, what do you need? Ironclad guarantees?"

"No. Just some more time to think this through, the way Henry suggested in his memo, The Decision Matrix."

"Okay. Let's do it and get on home. It's getting late."

It took the group an hour, but, as a subdivision of Part 3, they put together the matrix shown in Exhibit 4. Here's what they did:

First, under Benefits, they listed all the positive consequences of each plan. Second, under Liabilities, they listed all the negative consequences they could anticipate. Third, they identified the costs—in actual dollars—of each plan.

Then, they used a rating scale to evaluate each benefit and liability of each plan. Each person in the group assigned her or his own value to the number. Whether you average the scores, as they did, or just list them makes no difference. They are averaged in the scenario just to simplify matters.

To simplify things even more, they used a 10-point-positive and a 10-point-negative scale and rated everything as either a 5 or a 10. However, your numbers should range up and down the scale.

They assigned positive points to benefits and negative points to liabilities, and they weighted the factors in terms of their effects.

Finally, they calculated the cost-benefit ratio of each plan. This ratio is expressed as a rating rather than in dollars and cents because the *value* of the cost matters more for deciding whether to spend the money than the dollar return itself. That figure is derived by adding together the total value in each plan and entering the sums in the Cost-Benefit column.

Here is a summary of instructions for making the final decisions or for reaching consensus.

Instructions for Making Implementation Decisions

1. Review decision matrix and assign values to each benefit, liability or cost.
2. Use a scale of 1 to 10 for positive values and -1 to -10 for negative values.

Exhibit 4. Simplified decision matrix.

Plan	Benefits	Value	Liabilities	Value	Cost*	Value	Cost Benefit
1	Move contracts fast.	5	Overload word processing	−10			
	Reduce logjam.	10	Remove quality controls	−10			
			Intangible costs	−5			
	Total value	15		−25	0	5	−5
2	Move contracts fast.	5	Remove quality controls	−10			
	Reduce logjam.	10	Intangible costs	−5			
	Total value	15		−15	0	5	5
3	Simplify procedures.	10	Requires time	−10			
	Improve methods.	10	Training needed	−5			
	In mainframe more quickly.	10	Equipment needed	−10	$17.5	−10	
	Reduce manual work.	10					
	Reduce errors.	10					
	Total value	50		−25	−10	−10	15

*Cost = Actual cash expenditures anticipated to implement plan

3. Total each column.
4. In the final, cost-benefit column, enter the sum of the columns. That figure identifies the value of the plan. The plan with the highest positive value should be the one you implement first, assigning a sunset date to the action.

"So, Di," Paula asked when they had finished their matrix. "What do you think?"

"The numbers speak for themselves. I guess I have to agree to Plan 3, as long as we set a date on which the sun goes down if it's not working."

"We all agreed to that," Dan responded.

"I still think I'm missing something, because I don't see how we're going to get all the program managers to use their PCs."

"I'm going to put my facilitator's hat back on," Dan interjected. "That's a different problem altogether. Have we reached consensus on the plan we're going to back?"

Diane answered first. "I suppose you're really asking me. You two wanted Plan 3 from the start."

"Do you have anything else to discuss—any qualms you want satisfied?"

"No. And, Dan, you're really doing this brainstorming thing well. I didn't think you had it in you."

"You know, I'm kinda enjoying myself, too."

Group problem solving can be fun, and handled right, it should be. At the same time, none of this suggests that all problems should be handled with this much depth or by a group. However, when a really thorny organizational-centered problem strikes, an in-depth organizational offense is the best defense. Here are some suggestions for successfully completing this offensive.

1. Using the outline of the worksheet shown in Exhibits 1–3, write up your own answers to the questions to be asked during the brainstorming session—*before* the meeting! Come prepared, and ask the other people involved to prepare themselves as well. If possible, distribute the outline of questions to the other people.
2. Discuss everyone's answers and arrive at a con-

sensus. You may not achieve consensus in one meeting if yours is a complex problem, but that's to be expected.

3. If the problem is complex and has a number of different parts, don't try to solve the problem in one sitting and with the entire group at one time. Break the problem into reasonable parts, and assign different people—either individually or in teams—different parts to work on. In short, don't try to eat your elephant in one gulp.

4. Reconvene the group on a designated date. You'll be pleasantly surprised to see how much everyone has to contribute to solving (1) the part on which they've been working and (2) the problem as a whole.

When a difficult, self-centered problem strikes, you can use the same techniques, sitting by yourself at your desk. Remember, all it takes is something on which to write and something to use for writing on it. Let the ideas flow; write down everything; don't censor yourself; and once you feel drained, stop.

Take a walk; get a cup of coffee or a soda pop; get away from your list of ideas. When you come back to it, you'll see it through fresher eyes.

Now be analytic: Look for repetitions or redundancies. Examine the possibilities or feasibility of your ideas. Use the decision matrix if necessary. That way, making a decision amounts to reaching a consensus with yourself.

Visualization

So, they solved the problems at Brown, Inc., right? Well, no. Not entirely.

Remember the situation identified among the indicators that some of the people, including Diane, were afraid of using their PCs or CRTs—what some people call computerphobia? That was still unresolved, and it's doubtful that any of the methods described here would help her solve that one.

Something else was called for, perhaps even an unusual method such as visualization. In a computerphobia type of situation, visualizing may be able to solve the problems by replacing a fear of the unknown with images of success.

Most people can visualize, although some don't know it. Those accustomed to living in a vertical world—analytic thinkers—can train themselves to visualize almost as well as lateral thinkers, and can even use visualization to "see" the connections that may have come unhinged in a straight-line problem. Visualization can also aid divergent thinking because, through visualization, a person can conceive of the impossible.

Visual imagery, giving free reign to your visual imagination, works best when working on self-centered problems, since it's a process in which the individual exercises complete control. The technique consists of nothing more than relaxing, closing your eyes, clearing your mind of all extraneous influences, and telling your own mind what to see. There's nothing to stop you from practicing this method while sitting at your desk.

Since the technique definitely doesn't suit everyone's management style, you should try it out for and by yourself before deciding to join a growing number of managers who use visualization to attack organizational-centered problems, especially diffuse problems. Some people think of visual imagery as a form of hypnosis, so I don't recommend your using it unless you and the people with you feel comfortable with it.

But it is another way to address problems, such as the one with which Diane still had to contend: getting over her own computerphobia and helping the employees who, for whatever reason, also resisted automation. Such fears don't respond to logic, exhortation, or threat. However, in the scenario, Plan 3 called for everyone to use the automated system.

Visual imagery helps people feel more comfortable with things that frighten them. Let's see what happened when Diane used it on herself. After reading a book that described the use of visual imagery as a relaxation and problem-solving technique, she took these steps.*

*See also, Donald H. Weiss, *Managing Stress* (New York: AMACOM, 1987), another book in the Successful Office Skills Series, which contains instructions and a script for the relaxation exercise described here.

First, with both feet flat on the floor and her hands folded in her lap, she closed her eyes. Then, she talked to herself about relaxing. At first, she used a tape recording to help talk herself down into a deep, relaxed state. Later, with practice, she was able to do it without a tape.

The tape gave these instructions:

When I tell you to do it, take a deep breath to signal yourself that it's okay to relax. When you take your deep breath, I'll count to 5 slowly, while you relax. Take a deep breath now and hold it: 1—2—3—4—5.

Slowly let out your breath as I count to 5. Exhale slowly: 1—2—3—4—5. Let yourself relax.

Listen to your breathing. Breathe normally and listen to yourself inhale and exhale. Let your muscles relax. Just listen to your breathing and relax. Now do that for a minute or two. Listen to your breathing and relax.

The tape became silent as Diane quietly listened to her own breathing and relaxed. Speaking very softly, the voice on the tape continued with the instructions:

Now that you're feeling more relaxed, remember how it feels to be this comfortable with yourself. When you're working to overcome a fear, some kind of anxiety, tell yourself that fear's natural, the mind's way of warning you to be cautious, to take care, and to protect yourself if necessary.

Then, Diane talked to herself about her fear of using a computer:

Many people feel uptight about using computers. So, it's okay that I feel tense about it, too. I'm not alone. A lot of people have given a lot of different reasons why, but *why* doesn't matter right now. I want to use the automated system. It's faster, more accurate, and more convenient for other people to access the files. Only if I relax with my computer will I get past some of my fears about it.

Now, with your eyes closed and while you're very relaxed and staying relaxed, look at a picture in your mind of you doing what you fear to do.

And Diane saw herself, in her mind, sitting in front of the computer.

She watched herself sitting there, working. She looked at the screen and saw what was there. She let the screen fill her mind—a worksheet for costing hotel accommodations. She watched herself pull up the rates for the Hilton in San Diego. In her mind, she entered "100 priority rooms and. . . ."

As she worked out the problem in her mind, Diane went through the steps of costing hotel accommodations for the program. When she was finished with her visualization, she slowly opened her eyes and carefully considered how it felt to successfully complete costing a program on the PC. "It felt pretty good," she decided. "It isn't as intimidating now as it seemed to be."

Sure, this is a story, but it dramatizes a technique used by many people for breaking through an irrational problem. This dramatization illustrates imagery connected with a specific problem, but visualizing fantasies with no apparent connection to the problem often helps also. The fantasies may suggest answers that don't come to mind without them.

Once more, it should be acknowledged that the technique is not for everyone. If you want to try it and would like to use it with the people reporting to you, use it on yourself first. Many relaxation tapes on the market will help you. See if you too can visualize the solution to a problem.

Review and Continuation

Regardless of the method you use for attacking your problems, end your plan with review dates to avoid a common reason for running into serious problems. In

Exhibit 5. Review.

Part 5:

1. Set a date for reviewing progress toward the plan's goals.

   Illustration

   November 30, 198x

2. List the acceptable targets for the indicators on the review date.

   Acceptable Targets

   - Fifteen days or more past signing date: 1
   - Almost fifteen days old: 3
   - Complaints at acceptable levels: 1
   - Sales commissions delayed over sixty days: 0
   - No increase in cancellations or rejections of terms

---

the scenario, the managers at Brown, Inc., had not known what was happening until much too late to prevent the upheaval they experienced.

Part 5, Review, shown in Exhibit 5, and Part 6, Continuation Decision, shown in Exhibit 6, are the points at which you prepare for the worst and plan for achieving the ideal. The exhibits illustrate a review and continuation decision plan. They set out the steps that Brown's supervisors *intend* to take.

When you complete your plans, set at least one review date on which you'll take a look at how well the plan is going. Depending on the problem and the plan, you may have to set more than one date. Of course, if you spot deviations from plans before a review date, you take corrective action as needed. Also identify what steps to take in the event something goes wrong with fulfilling the plan.

Exhibit 6. Continuation decision.

Part 6

What will you do if the plan implemented does not achieve the desired results?

> *Illustration*
>
> · Unless we are close to achieving Plan 3's objectives, implement Plan 2.

Sometimes, however, people let their problems become crises, although they can see their egg is endangered. Sometimes, they don't want to admit that they have a problem. They don't want to deal with the symptoms, let along the causes: "If we don't deal with it, maybe it'll go away on its own."

That's what Dan wanted to do. But, the world doesn't work that way. Once an egg starts to teeter, look out below!

Conclusion

Eggs break all the time, but up to this point, I've been talking about what to do after an egg falls and shatters.

When you wait until the indicators become too severe to ignore, you're engaged in reactive problem solving, a necessary but often frustrating way to go about coping with your work situation. Putting out fires, supervisors say, makes up over 75 percent of their workload. Most people have to salvage their efforts to achieve their goals through reactive methods because they wait for the problems to occur or to reach crisis proportions before taking steps to prevent them in the first place.

Effective managers begin with the proposition that no plan is free from possible disaster, and they produce plans for taking corrective action when necessary. They know they can't anticipate every contingency or recognize every danger, so they describe the ideal situation, or at least an acceptable one, and, over time, they measure reality against the plan. By making these comparisons, they're able to identify problems or dangers as they are occurring and take steps to correct the situation before anything serious happens.

That is *proactive* management, as distinguished from reactive management. Proactive managers plan for problems, solving them on paper or in simulations before they happen. In this form of problem solving—*worst-case planning*—before anything happens at all, you decide what to do in the event that something endangers the plan.

When you sense that something is wrong, needed, or wanted, doing nothing about it is itself an action—a negative action that could accelerate the danger to what you're doing. Only positive, affirmative steps toward salvaging your plan will make that discomfort or dissatisfaction go away.

INDEX

About the Author

Donald H. Weiss, Ph.D., of Millers' Mutual Insurance in Alton, Illinois, has been engaged in education and training for over 26 years and has written numerous articles, books, audio cassette/workbook programs, and video training films on effective sales and supervisory or management skills. He speaks regularly on stress management and other personal development subjects, and has produced a variety of related printed or recorded materials.

During his career, Dr. Weiss has been the Manager of Special Projects for a training and development firm, the Manager of Management Training for an insurance company, the Director of Training for an employment agency group, a training consultant, and a writer-producer-director of video training tapes. He also has taught at several universities and colleges in Texas, including the University of Texas at Arlington and Texas Christian University, in Fort Worth.

Currently, Dr. Weiss is Corporate Training Director for Millers' Mutual Insurance.